BULLDOZERS
PUSH!

by Beth Bence Reinke

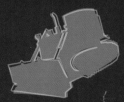

BUMBA BOOKS™

LERNER PUBLICATIONS ◆ MINNEAPOLIS

Note to Educators:

Throughout this book, you'll find critical thinking questions. These can be used to engage young readers in thinking critically about the topic and in using the text and photos to do so.

Lerner Publications Company
A division of Lerner Publishing Group, Inc.
241 First Avenue North
Minneapolis, MN 55401 USA

For reading levels and more information, look up this title at www.lernerbooks.com.

Library of Congress Cataloging-in-Publication Data

Names: Reinke, Beth Bence, author.
Title: Bulldozers push! / by Beth Bence Reinke.
Description: Minneapolis : Lerner Publications, [2017] | Series: Bumba books™—Construction zone | Audience: Age 4–7. | Audience: Grade K to Grade 3. | Includes bibliographical references and index.
Identifiers: LCCN 2016041006 (print) | LCCN 2016050322(ebook) | ISBN 9781512433586 (lb : alk. paper) | ISBN 9781512455403 (pb : alk. paper) | ISBN 9781512450200 (eb pdf)
Subjects: LCSH: Bulldozers—Juvenile literature.
Classification: LCC TA725 .R44 2017 (print) | LCC TA725 (ebook) | DDC 629.225—dc23

LC record available at https://lccn.loc.gov/2016041006

Manufactured in the United States of America
1—CG—7/15/17

LERNER
SOURCE

Expand learning beyond the printed book. Download free, complementary educational resources for this book from our website, www.lernerresource.com.

Table of
Contents

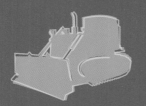

Bulldozers

Bulldozers are strong machines.

They push dirt, rocks, and other things.

They clear land at construction sites.

What else might a bulldozer push?

Bulldozers do not have wheels.

They drive on tracks.

Tracks grip the earth.

A bulldozer drives forward.

It pushes things with

its blade.

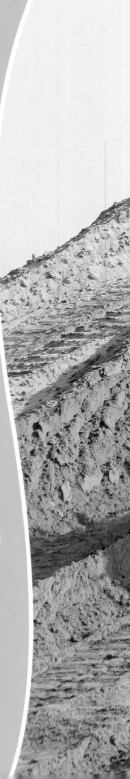

A driver sits in the cab.

The blade is on the front.

The blade scrapes the ground

as it pushes.

The bulldozer makes a smooth path.

It clears the way for a new road.

Why do roads need a smooth path?

ripper

Some bulldozers have a ripper.

The ripper rips and digs up soil.

It can make a ditch.

What else might a ripper help dig?

A bulldozer works

in the woods.

It clears trees.

Now workers can

build a house.

Some bulldozers move trash

at dumps.

Others help push snow.

Bulldozers push lots of things.

They clear spaces to get the job done.

Parts of a Bulldozer

cab

ripper

blade

tracks

Picture Glossary

construction sites

places where construction, or building, takes place

ditch

a long, narrow hole in the dirt

ripper

a claw on the back of a bulldozer used for ripping up land

tracks

belts that move a bulldozer over the ground

23

Read More

Meister, Cari. *Bulldozers.* Minneapolis: Bullfrog Books, 2014.

Osier, Dan. *Bulldozers.* New York: PowerKids, 2014.

Reinke, Beth Bence. *Front Loaders Scoop!* Minneapolis: Lerner Publications, 2018.

Index

Photo Credits